Psalms of Gratitude and Prayer

PSALMS
of
GRATITUDE
and
PRAYER

poems by
JOHN J. BRUGALETTA

RESOURCE *Publications* • Eugene, Oregon

PSALMS OF GRATITUDE AND PRAYER

Copyright © 2016 John J. Brugaletta. All rights reserved. Except for brief quotations in critical publications or reviews, no part of this book may be reproduced in any manner without prior written permission from the publisher. Write: Permissions, Wipf and Stock Publishers, 199 W. 8th Ave., Suite 3, Eugene, OR 97401.

Resource Publications
An Imprint of Wipf and Stock Publishers
199 W. 8th Ave., Suite 3
Eugene, OR 97401

www.wipfandstock.com

PAPERBACK ISBN: 978-1-5326-0247-4
HARDCOVER ISBN: 978-1-5326-0249-8
EBOOK ISBN: 978-1-5326-0248-1

Manufactured in the U.S.A.   08/15/16

In memory of
Eugene Montague
who taught me what
a poem can do

Contents

Acknowledgments | ix

Introduction | xi
Itadaki Masu | xiii

Gratitude
Before Praying | 3
The Present | 4
Better than Best | 5
The Benefits of Pain | 6
Distractions at Prayer | 7
Disaffirmation | 9
Bouquet | 10
The Lump of Clay to the Potter | 11
The Comics Page | 12
Tract for Houseguests at the Emperor's Estate | 13
Four More Beatitudes | 15
Fruit | 16
One out of Ten | 17
Broken Promise | 18
Christmas | 19
The Risk in Releasing | 21
Seeing | 22
Windows | 23
Acrobats | 24

Grace
Dancing with God | 27
First Aid | 29
Gem | 30
Courting | 31
Circular | 32
Tulips | 33
Lent | 34

Age | 35
Fall, Winter, Spring | 36
Petitions | 37
Nightsong | 38
Seer | 39
The Kingdom Comes | 40
Eucharist | 41
Teach Us to Pray | 42

Generosity
Side by Side | 47
The Flowering of Evil | 48
House of Injuries | 49
David and Judith | 50
Charles the Great | 51
Postcards from Chaos | 52
Preparation of the Bed | 53
Working | 54
Kiss | 55
Lent II | 56

Wisdom
Everything Is Otherwise | 61
Fox Sparrow | 62
Awe | 63
Well Water | 64
Born Again | 65
Containers | 66
Belief | 68
CPAP | 70
Purpose | 71
Oracular Meddling | 73
Don Quixote the Chickadee | 74
Silence | 75
Led into the Wilderness | 77
Surprised by the Ease of It | 78
Yes, No, and Neither | 80
Naming the Logos | 81
Finis | 82
Proper Prophet | 83

Acknowledgments

The following poems were previously published as indicated, some of them in an earlier form:

"Acrobats"	*The Lamp-Post*
"Containers"	*The Lamp-Post*
"Christmas"	*Time of Singing*
"Everything Is Otherwise"	*Relief**
"Finis"	*The Lyric*
"Fox Sparrow"	*Anglican Theological Review*
"Itadaki Masu"	*Relief* *
"Metamorphosis"	*The Penwood Review*
"Naming the Logos"	*National Catholic Reporter*
"Proper Prophet"	*Christianity and Literature*
"Teach Us to Pray"	*Image*
"The Blinding"	*The Penwood Review*

* Because they were especially appropriate to this volume, "*Itadaki Masu*" and "Everything Is Otherwise" have also been reprinted here from *With My Head Rising out of the Water*, by John J. Brugaletta. Negative Capability Press, 2014.

Introduction

"[The teachers of the law] devour widows' houses and for a show make lengthy prayers. Such men will be punished most severely."

Mark 12 – 40

"Thoughts are but coins. Let me not trust, instead
Of Thee, their thin-worn image of Thy head."

C.S. Lewis

Itadaki Masu*

I have received water, flowing and pooled, salt and fresh,
>cold and hot; wind off the ocean, among the trees,
>over wheat fields; wool for warmth.

I am grateful for these, and for the many-touching octopi,
>the common beauty of oleanders, tough-limbed
>oaks, lithe ocelots, leather-skinned oranges, and
>pungent onions.

About me lie perch from farm ponds, peppers and parsnips,
>potatoes and tellicherry peppercorns, pork and
>peaches, paprika, together with the sweet sadness
>of Pachelbel.

I have been given air to breathe, alders leafing out in spring,
>crisp apples, deep-flavored apricots, and the shield-
>like leaves of aspidistras.

Grapes and goldfinches, garlic and grass are in my treasury;
>jackrabbits and jays, ginger and juncos have come
>to me as gifts.

I am inebriated on biscuits and bass, bread and bears,
>bicycles and barracudas, on basil and brass.

Clouds and rainfall, snow and sleet, sunshine and darkness
>are my blessings, as are moonlight and firelight,
>starlight and candlelight.

I have been awarded Mozart and Bach, Verdi and Puccini,
>Homer and Shakespeare, Thomas More and Martin
>Luther, Herbert and Donne.

I have received from on high appreciative dogs and dignified
>housecats, deer and raccoons, chickens and grosbeaks,
>friendship and children, fuchsias and dahlias, soil,
>stone and steel.

* *Japanese: "I have received from on high."*

May I never be ungrateful for any shelter, any mouthful of food or sip of water, any friendly gesture, any offer of help, any touch of understanding.

Gratitude

"So then, just as you received Christ Jesus as Lord, continue to live in him, rooted and built up in him, strengthened in the faith as you were taught, and overflowing with thankfulness."

COLOSSIANS 2—6

"There are minds so impatient of inferiority that their gratitude is a species of revenge."

SAMUEL JOHNSON

Before Praying

Like a farmer come from hens and hogs,
his hands befouled, his feet two mounds of mud,
who stands before the door and thinks himself
too filthy for clean floor and fragrant table,

I come to You with desecrated phrase
made foul by those who think their lies a skill,
and timid creatures who think lies are kind.
What honest words are left to speak to You?

But with Your guidance I have found a well
to wash my hands and rinse my smelly mouth,
and then, before I pray, take off my boots.
Only fools defile a holy place.

The Present

Small as I was, possessing like a king,
I knew my property came from my dad,
and not just some of mine, but everything.
What could I give him that he had not had?

The possibilities became a list
with statues first, then windows, then
his picture that I daily blessed and kissed.
But these were feeble objects made by men.

With Christmas drawing near, my next thought flew
to duties, proper acts of charity,
to hordes converted (to my rivals' few).
Yet which of these could I say came from me?

At last I found the box my gift would fill
and put inside the best I had, my will.

Better than Best

This little church
that lives by slip and lurch
will sing off-key
and seldom will agree.

But these are yours and work for You,
and though their tones may be somewhat askew,
as amateurs, they love You so
that all their songs may not impress with polished show.

We howl and growl to serenade our artful God.
You do not think it odd
that those You made should be so artless in their hymns,
for they must use their limbs

to till the social fields of sullen earth
and bring to birth
a fair facsimile of heaven's town
and your renown.

Like men who dig, and wives who press,
who love their children nonetheless,
and touch their faces with a hand
abrasive but as soft as sand,
they honor You with secondary gifts,
which, better than the best, may patch all rifts.

The Benefits of Pain

Now comes my pain that sweeps away the world.
The cluttered workday, all the social weights,
the habit that compels on mindless day—
all gone, or hid, like minor creatures when
a monarch makes approach. The pinpoint distant
star, confronted so immense, becomes the sun,
and I am intimate with You, and dead,
for no one lives this close to all that is.

My gratitude to You who send such pain,
who melt our eyes to let us see the real,
who break our legs so we will sit and think,
who scorch our tongues so we may speak alone
of You, think none but You, see who we are
by seeing we are not the God of all.

Distractions at Prayer

Hear me, Lord, secluded here
in this closed and quiet place.
Surely You attend our prayers
anywhere we call to You.
Still, the human mind, it seems,
wavers like a candle flame,
moved aside by every hiss,
upward and intent on You
only when the air is still.

Pain and anguish forge their own
upright highway to your home,
but our daily talk desires
isolation and the calm
of a pair who sit and talk,
all their children now asleep.

Hear me, Lord, my nagging chores
set aside to be performed
when You've filled my lungs with life.
Needs of family and friends
will not draw my thoughts from You
if I hold them to your eyes.

Now the thick, diurnal dust
of a thousand minor aches,
with a hundred pinprick jabs,
umbrage taken, nurtured close—
now I ask You clear away.

Either pull them from my soul,
or if it be more your will,
let my inward ear be deaf
to their buzzing. Let me be
wholly focused on our talk
here in this secluded place,
here where holiness resides
for the moment, for this day.

Disaffirmation

Why is my head a stone, my heart dry wood?
Have I drunk poison and am paralyzed?
Once towering, how am I now downsized?
I creep and crouch who early marched and stood.

These are declining days of febrile light,
of wizened biceps, quadriceps of wax.
A desperate inhabitant of shacks,
I have misplaced my attitude and height.

It may be for the best. I've died before,
or almost did: on mountain roads, in slums;
when pocket-poor, while feeding on scant crumbs,
and sizing up for taste the shoes I wore.

But now at least I'm grateful for this least:
my height now grown by having been decreased.

Bouquet

This pink and yellow messenger of scent
is in its seventh day and sags.
But if its lovely form is spent,
its gift remains and rises from these rags.

The vase around it stands the same and still,
and offers water like our God.
But roses decompose until
we sniff their memory and think, "How odd."

How odd that something permanent should take
such pains for temporary bliss.
And yet this vase stands for their sake
and holds their beauty like a lifted kiss.

The Lump of Clay to the Potter

When You slap me onto the wheel's exact center
with your accurate eye, then set me dizzying around,
may I not wobble, but sit still as I spin fast.
When You insert your thumbs to open my mouth,
may I yawn the perfect O of the perfect prayer.

When You touch me both outside and inside at once,
lifting me up, making me upright but more fragile,
may I not collapse into an ashtray, but stand
as your cereal bowl, your vegetable server,
or, if You will, even a vase, a casserole, a teapot.

May there be no pockets in me to expand in the kiln,
for your other pots may be shattered if I explode.
May we all serve at your table, meekly waiting
for your eye, your hand to lift us, your lip to sup.

The Comics Page

Their week is black and white, as if they slid
back every Monday to that wintry scene
before a technicolor screen had bloomed.
They're cabined also in a meager space,
obeying rules against more room or joy.

But then on Sunday all their lives are changed.
The lawns and Blondie's dress are green as hope;
the sky above Prince Valiant is pure blue.
Page after page is spread and packed with hues
like flower beds in spring, or bowls of eggs
dyed pink or mauve, yellow or chartreuse
to celebrate the new red blood of life.

Tract for Houseguests at the Emperor's Estate

Remember always that you do not own the house.
If this fact causes you to be less careful
with its structure or its contents,
you will not be looked upon favorably.

While you may at decent intervals suggest wiser behavior
on the part of other guests, it is not your role to expel them.
The Emperor has better ways of doing so than you do.

When you are first seated at table,
your manners will be crude and offensive to other guests,
as well as to His Majesty.
This should not throw you into despair,
but it should shame you enough to learn better behavior.
Among other things,
this means never taking food from your neighbor's plate,
or drinking from her cup,
or throwing your bones in his direction.

If the servants are negligent in serving hungry guests,
you are expected to rise,
even from a place of honor,
and fetch their food yourself.
Do not be surly in this,
for the task is a higher honor than the place you rose from.

Avoid at all costs
the grave error of
accepting the Emperor's hospitality
without giving it a thankful thought.
It was given you freely,

and your freely-given gratitude
will be a sign of your soul's health.

Speak little of yourself.
There are many others
better than you who remain silent.

Four More Beatitudes

Glory be to God for unsuccess,
for houses that fall down and jobs that quit.
They teach us what we'd be without our hands.

Give thanks for planned societies and fads
that promise blissful lives then fizzle out.
They show that we could never make the world.

Love lofty titles tacked on menial jobs.
They lend bright uniforms then leave us bare
to demonstrate how thin as gauze is pride.

Be grateful when your children bring you shame.
Admit your disappointment helps you learn
they had to fail, for you and we have failed.

Fruit

The raindrops on December's cherry tree
are far too many to perceive at once.
It figures forth my life—that there should be
so many blessings on so many fronts.

As each one glistens in the winter light,
a thought arrives and enters like an axe:
My tree bears nothing that a tooth can bite.
These liquid jewels mock what my life lacks.

I kneel (as if the gardener had cut
me down for fruitlessness) and ask to bear
two apricots, one plum, a hazel nut.
That's when I hear Him shock the shining air:

"What you produce is not your own but Mine.
I gave these drops and light them by design."

One out of Ten

Now that the days I might have followed You
are mostly dissolute and wasted on
a sensate bliss turned woe when bliss was gone,
I offer moments for the years You're due.

I see You take them and forget the rest,
and from my thankfulness my fondness sprouts
engulfing me in greater bliss than doubts
could ever have afforded me at best.

But like a widower who weds again,
I see my old conjunction's portrait near,
which pilfers my new life and keeps it poor.

You are my second language and my cure.
I beg You teach me. I'll soon reach my bier.
Then I'll be fluent one year out of ten.

Broken Promise

What is accomplished in a mayfly's time?
They eat, they rest, they try to mate; that's all.
And we who live the decades' pantomime?
Our fruits of life proportionately small,
when death is near we cast about like Saul
to find out why our promises had gleamed
if in the end delivery wore a pall.
Why do our fates not hold to what they seemed?

How shall we live so that our days may climb
the circling stairs and never slip and fall?
A moment's altitude persuades us the sublime
must be our proper state; we shall not crawl.
It takes one fool enticing us to brawl
to make us lose all that our pride had schemed,
forget our talents and forsake our call.
Why does fate never hold to what it seemed?

Those honors paid us in our laurelled prime
have soured on the tree and turned to gall.
Where now are those who took as paradigm
our every word and act, and promised all?
The rooms are still, no candles in the hall
where recently our cordial fellows teemed
(though I had spied a handprint on the wall).
Why cannot fate be true to what it seemed?

You smile, my King, and I too smile and scrawl,
for now I know the truth, that I'm esteemed,
that You've reversed herein my fated fall.
Thank God our fates won't hold to what they seemed.

Christmas

The earth's now near
that point of year
when Christmas is observed.
The fir tree leans,
the clan convenes
and housewives are unnerved.

There's goose and ham
and lots of Spam
so no one nice will starve.
Our Uncle Bob
has lost his job,
so mother lets him carve.

A toddler shrieks.
A baby leaks.
It's bedlam, there's no doubting.
There's so much noise
of spats and toys
it's useless even shouting.

At any rate
we celebrate
and that's the way we do it.
It's aches and pains,
and then joy wanes
so once more we renew it.

But something swell
rings like a bell
when sunlight's at its weakest.

The cosmos reels,
a church bell peals,
and strongest comes as meekest.

The Risk in Releasing

As I watch the naturalist with his lopsided grin
explain to my living room how these cheetah cubs
were adopted by a lioness, how they raised them,
taught them to live on their own, saw one killed by
another lioness, took the survivor to a refuge, a walled
garden, a place with no risks, only a stultifying security—
when I heard his sadness for the remaining cat
let out to the dangerous quest for fulfillment—

I thought of that ancient garden, too ancient
to seem real to us, but a potential disaster for us all,
a sanitized room to grow flabby and stupid in,
a room to remain a child into weakness and wrinkles,
and I became thankful for threats that can be overcome,
diseases that might be healed, catastrophes to survive,
losses perhaps redeemed, death defeated,
as well as understanding better that Naturalist
who made the painful but good choice for us.

Seeing

The ancient shamans sought to harmonize
a sick one's spirit with the sky and earth
so that a little lameness or imperfect eyes
could not compare with marriage, love, and birth.

It seemed no longer that one did not fit
with rain and lightning, rattlesnakes and deer.
He took a little dust, and then he spit
into it, made some mud. . .. Their eyes would clear.

The universe is both an infinite
incomprehensibility and home,
a well-worn pair of shoes that always fit;
one's heart is either warm or metronome.

There is a living One who offers life.
Why should we offer Him, blade first, a knife?

Windows

All homes have windows, but where curses fly,
anxiety erodes, or appetite prevails,
we use them only to detect a spy,
suspected neighbors, or approaching gales.

And so because of our unease we're blind
to graceful cats, Dutch irises, the toys
that symbolize a childhood's tranquil mind.
We cannot hear for our internal noise.

But when we've seen we have no need to curse,
that we are safe enough, and have been fed,
then we can smell and taste delicious bread.
Desiring less, we have a gold-filled purse.
Some gratitude for table and a bed
will soothe our bruises better than a nurse.

Acrobats

Let's all pray for acrobats,
Whose feet, like goddesses', transcend
The earth like pert aristocrats'
And start up toward where eagles end.

A careful foot, at angle just,
Possesses wire ten yards above
In what appears as gripping lust
But really what amounts to love.

Up high where just one slip would break
A collar bone, a leg or head,
One juggles plates for baby's sake,
Who's napping safely in her bed.

And then, eliciting more awe,
He rides the wire upon a bike
While holding on his upraised jaw
His partner, trustful as a tyke,

Who, in her turn, holds wide a bar,
A beach ball resting on each end.
Let's pray no wicked wind will mar
This lovely gift they have and lend.

For all of us are acrobats
Who juggle gratitude and tasks
While wearing shakily six hats
And try to do what heaven asks.

Grace

"All . . . are justified freely by [God's] grace through the redemption that came by Christ Jesus."

Romans 3 — 23–24

"The feelings we receive from our spiritual life are the least of its benefits. The invisible and unfelt grace of God is much greater, and it is beyond our comprehension."

John of the Cross

Dancing with God

"When you were under the fig tree I saw you."

I sat against the wall beside a plant
and peeked through branches at the lovely ones
who hardly touched the floor, their steps so light.
The Prince would dance with one and then would change
His partner so no beauty would be left
untouched at hand and in the small of back.

He looked at me. He saw me there behind
my potted plant and looked right through my eyes.
And so I turned them on the floor below
my ugly feet so He would never see
again my envy and my festering.
Then He was there. He stood in front of me.

"Come," He said. My mouth could not say no.
He took my hand and led me out among
the comeliness and grace that filled the room.
At first I stood and waited for my Prince
to move my feet and make me glide with grace,
but He said, "You must follow me, and that
means you must act as well, in step with me."

At times we turned so I could see my plant,
the chair behind it with another girl
who looked between the leaves and seemed to hope.
I knew He saw her looking, and in time
He asked her too to dance. And dance they did,
and I was joyful for the two of us.

While staring at them and remembering,
I saw her plain, clean countenance become
as beautiful as other girls who danced,
so looked into a glass and saw myself
a belle. And then I knew all beauty comes
from love, and from the Source of all the loves.

First Aid

What I have done to You, if I had done
to any ordinary mortal man,
would have obtained his lifelong enmity,
his plans to blast my family from life,
to leave me chained to coyotes and the ants
and curse me till he's spent his dying breath.

But You, my God, perceived in me a pale
and feeble gleam of good You lent at first.
You breathed on that weak spark until
the voices of my friends returned like bells,
and then I had just strength enough to turn
face down and abject as I begged your eye
see none of my offenses, and your ear
detect no slander from my wagging tongue.

When I had asked, I felt a cosmic nod;
You had consented to your own demand.

Gem

There are no guarantees that bliss will come,
not for a lifetime or a year or day.
A chance misunderstanding makes us glum
then real affection blows our clouds away.

The weather of our minds is our bequest,
a gift of trust in our stability,
the trust that we will see the earth's a nest,
a home of relative tranquility.

And yet He hears our cries and blesses them
as He blessed Jesus' wail upon the cross.
We are not born to see each day a gem
but to retain our faith amid our loss.

He is the gem, and not the world's delights,
to which we have no predetermined rights.

Courting

An awkward youth, I longed for what I lacked:
a graceful motion, quiet certitude.
I found these—bits and pieces—in my friends
and certain girls before whom I might kneel.

And now that I am old I still desire
my missing parts, my absent energies,
but now they've grown so large that I can see
no mouth, can hear no voice that satisfies.

I understand at last. Those glints of light
in others like myself were spoor You left
as You transformed base elements into
these forms that fascinate our youthful eyes.

It would betray a cruelty You lack
to dazzle us and then discard our loves.

Circular

Funny how when the light goes you begin to drowse,
then, a second later, time starts again and it's light.
You'd think time would move unwavering and non-stop,
but no, it turns, and dies, and comes back suddenly
into sight like a playful parent with a giggling child.

And light, when it takes its farewell, goes wide
in a circle so huge that it qualifies as a straight line,
returning much used but none the staler for that.

This crusty sphere we stand on, the water falling fresh
on our gardens, bear cubs sniffing their way into the world—
each donates its voice, timid or loud, piping or profound,
to one chorale, the libretto in a language we've forgotten,
with a meaning we've known since before we were born.

Tulips

Bit by bit the tulips open,
candy yellow, candy red,
shocking us with sudden brilliance,
then one day they all are dead.

Poets sing their dreary passing,
turning substance into song,
but an April thwarts their wailing,
proving all they knew was wrong.

What had seemed to us enchanting
was a moment's sharp delight.
When it fell, it went on living
deep in soil and out of sight.

Here and there the world holds letters
only thinking comprehends.
Eyes see patterned marks on paper
never wondering who sends.

Thinking sees the brilliant yellow
as the crust of hallowed bread,
and the grape as, in its essence,
wholesome and a hearty red.

Bit by bit the message opens.
Word by word we understand.
Spring by spring the tulips flourish
till they resurrect the land.

Lent

A tolework sky allows the light to pass
through scattered pinpricks to this sooty world,
each tiny aperture a prophet's mouth.

The lunar, jaundiced face illuminates
like hired help—a joyless character
pretending it's the source itself of light.

And then the sun, or something very like.
And every time he comes he's just in time,
the fields dispirited, the maples ghosts,
the sheep and humans huddled for their lives.

Just when our hope is flickering and wan,
the world become a paper silhouette,
he rises in the east and warms our day
with light to walk by for a little year.

Age

Give me, Lord, the grace to say
Thank you for this breaking day.
Though my back and legs may ache,
Still I live and stir awake.
Though my interests pale and dry,
I have glimpsed the reason why:

Soon this thin and fragile earth
Must be shed as afterbirth.
Those who cannot leave its womb
Must remain in growing gloom.

Aches and lack of interest aid
When the time has come to trade
Goblet, merriment and tome
For that much more joyful home
Where our Father's will is done
And we pity mindless fun.

Let me learn at spreading dawn
How to leave behind what's gone.
Quicken my delight in You.
Make my aged spirit new.

Fall, Winter, Spring

Forgive our infidelity to You.
Our independence itched, and when we scratched,
the rank hyena who had promised it
commanded that we kiss the tracks he left:

An utter loyalty to clan and *patria,*
the view in all directions that we "own,"
the minted signs of worth that mount for us,
the sense that we're in charge and all obey.

We kissed them one or all, and doing so,
turned traitors to your friendship and your care.

Yet still the earth rotated and revolved,
still the rains descended, still the crops
produced in season and our children grew,
all orders You maintained to save our kind
despite our treason and the scorn implied.

You saw it as our immaturity
I'm sure, for otherwise the task were slight
to turn your face away and let us die.

Receive us now that we return to You.
We cannot mend the damage that we've done,
but we can recognize our flaw and know
where present loyalty has been repaid.

Petitions

I asked that He forgive my pestering his ear
with loud, repentant cries at old offenses.
And then, boor that I am, requested more of Him:
a life of comfort and prosperity
for family, for friends, for all the world beside.

"That little?" He replied. "And nothing more?"
Abashed at what I took as irony, I closed
my mouth and waited for his flames, or chill.
"What more?" He asked again, and I took heart to say,
"Your will in lieu of mine, if this is not
presumptuous of me." He nodded and was gone.

Nightsong

The light that bathed the world has gone away.
All things are wrapped in sleep, close kin to death,
and we, like mourners, doubt the coming day.
When will the Lord lend us his rousing breath?
Give us, Spirit, quickened hearts,
wisdom that your breath imparts.

We're told the planet turned its back upon
our source of light, that star we call the sun,
yet still it blazes though we feel it's gone
and feel the same about the Father's Son.
We believe You're at the door;
help us to believe it more.

A father holds his child's small hand to teach
it how to walk, until the toddler can.
That's when he watches, standing out of reach.
Our trust in absence is the Father's plan.
Dignity replaces fear
when we sense that You are near.

Seer

A man whose lips were blue, not from the cold
but from the words his septic spirit belched,
heard circling eagles screeching, "Read, read,"
and, opening a book, could see no print.

Instead the pages were of glass and showed
himself repellant, everything he loathed.
The screeches then transmuted to "Now speak,"
and he felt told to dance on broken legs.

He pleaded to be passed, but all that came
was an insane and molten heat that seared
his lips, his tongue, his larynx and his lungs.
Thus truly crippled, he began to sing,
which healed the cauterizing for his words.

The Kingdom Comes

In early light the darker shapes seem new,
resembling nothing we have seen before.
"Perturbing apparitions, what are you?"
I ask of clothing and the room's decor.

But soon the seeming endless task erodes
attention's patience, and I close my eyes.
When I awake the sun has broken codes
to demonstrate how immature my why's.

First light must be, I think, a space
to practice hope and recollect a face.

Eucharist

*Even the dogs eat the crumbs that fall
from their master's table.*

I hear above me plates, utensils, glasses.
Their clatter punctuates the talk one uses
while eating common meals. And as time passes,
here fall the crumbs each careful diner loses.

Say I'm a dog; why give me taste for blessing
if I'm to live on what the blest are spilling?
(The stained glass sparkles; why is it so depressing?
The hymn is hearty, but the air is chilling.)

The falsely wise say feelings never count,
but in this dryness I can hear the fount
that never fails, although it seems to move.

It tells me that you never disapprove
of change, so long as it is toward your feet,
when you will lift me up and let me eat.

Teach Us to Pray

after Thomas Merton

When you pray, let your tongue
taste the words it forms,
and let your mind watch the meanings forming.
This will paralyze your prayers,
but it will stop your meaningless recitations.

Next, as you pray to God,
think about his omniscience, his power,
his goodness and the problem of theodicy.
This too will stifle your prayers but,
done at other times, will cause you to pray.

Then, in times of prayer, think of your problems,
your dread of the coming day's tests,
of chores, illnesses and duties.
You may turn these distractions into petitions,
but alone they will not be satisfactory prayers.

This brings one to the asking of favors
on behalf of ourselves, our friends and the church.
This is something, but it is not enough,
for it is not focused directly upon God.
Still, even a little to One so great is much.

And then you may see through your prayer
as through a clean window, not seeing the window
but seeing God's mercy, and in that his love,
watching him adopt you as his child,
wretched child though you have been and are.

Yet still you see yourself as you pray,
and then you long to disappear, to see only God,
for your prayers no longer bring consolation
and you acknowledge for the first time that
you never loved him, but actually loved yourself.

For your love for God was a miserly love,
doled out in complacency, false modesty, conceit.
You were too self-confident, ignoring your self-delusions,
unafraid of being called a person of prayer.
Now you are terrified, and you finally regret your sins.

And now you pray, expecting nothing.
Now your pride has evaporated in the aridity.
Now any crumb of the stalest spiritual bread satisfies,
even surprises you that God should attend to you.
Now you truly pray, without knowing what you are saying.

Generosity

"The wicked borrow and do not repay, but the righteous give generously."
PSALM 37—21

"There's no delight in owning anything unshared."
SENECA

Side by Side

When I've moved on from here
I will remember these calm days,
the shady aconite,
the slender-legged deer,
the cherry trees
that graze on both
dark loam and sunlight.

I'll be nostalgic for the hours
spent nudging and aligning what
the Maker gave,
collaboration mingling us
so what is his is ours.
All palpable things
are like an arch through
which He seems diaphanous.

And knowing this, I almost see
his finger pointing to the needs:
weeding or a fence,
diplomacy or changing oil.
At times He will agree
they were just weeds.
At others I can sense
I've been mistaken in my toil.

But always He is there.
We make a curious pair.

The Flowering of Evil

"His spirit alone was Christian. His heart and mind
remained empty." Anatole France on Baudelaire

Let us pray for Charles Baudelaire,
for every wastrel merits Christian care.
His "giantess," for sake of argument,
let's say was oedipal, despite intent.

And let's concede religion was a game
he dabbled in to make himself a name.
St. Wystan may be right—he may have turned
the final second of his life and learned.

So let's petition heaven he be saved
no matter how heretically he raved.
For time in heaven is not like our own;
he may not yet have reached damnation's zone.

Let's ask that in that promised world there be
a padded dwelling place for such as he.
But please be careful—rise not from your knee
before you have appended this last plea:

No matter with what vigor they repent,
forbear to make such madmen president.

House of Injuries

I too dislike churchgoing,
the words mouthed but
unregistered or unmeant,
the dressing to impress
(either lavish or tattered),
excellence treated as
a diminution of others,
petty criticism for the sake
of self-advertisement.

But of course that is
the purpose of it all:
the chance to recognize
ourselves as one of those;
to see with a pang that
we are just as maimed
as any of the others;
that we belong with them.

And furthermore, that
the world has been
turned upside-down—
those who think they are
fine are, but on the outside,
and those of us
who admit our scars
just might be war heroes.

David and Judith

When David, young and ruddy, heard the threat
Goliath posed King Saul and Israel,
he offered to remove the giant pest
as handily as he had often killed
the predators that ate his father's sheep.
One rounded stone, set whirling in a sling,
flew out and crushed the brain's soft shape.
And then the giant's sword's beheading clang.
The grown and battle-hardened warriors
were bested by a boy in God's command.

And Judith, widow, living posh indoors,
went out—instead of all her fighting men—
to outmaneuver their top general
until his wine-besotted head, adoze,
lay pillowed and convenient for the kill,
defeating his whole army with two blows.
Bethulia had agreed to drop their arms,
to offer up their town (and Israel)
should God not help them on their terms.

In just such times the weakest must do all.

Charles the Great

"When the traitors had been hanged, Charles the Great
had the pagan Brandimonie Christened Juliane,
then took to his bed, ordered the bed curtains closed,
and slept. Down through the bed's canopy dove
Gabriel, declaiming, 'Charles, wake up. Arise and don
your royal garb. Christ's body needs you. Rise up, I say!'

"But Charles had taken to his bed for the last time.
'Oh, God,' he prayed in his dream, 'You have seen my life,
that every decision and every deed drinks my spirit.'
Then Charles the Great pulled at his long white beard
and wept unceasing, until he lay cold as stone."

Always when we are most tired, most regretful, most shamed,
our muscles shrunken and sore, our will wizened—
when we avoid praying for strength, fearing an answer—
always when we would fall on our knees to a worm
if we thought it would give us rest, unending rest—
it is always then that the Ruler of All Things sends a message
saying we are needed, now most of all, and desperately.

Then we can see that our earlier heroics, our brave rhetoric,
our kindnesses and loyalties and pains all were exercises,
preparations for this. If Charlemagne failed in the end,
he is not the only one to do so. Strictly speaking,
we are all at our worst when we are needed most.

Postcards from Chaos

It was on a day like this that the earth
shook Lisbon to the ground and
scandalized Voltaire into writing *Candide*.

It was on a day like this that the New Madrid
broke, changing the course of the Mississippi,
leaving a few stagnant lakes where it had run.

It was on a day like this that San Francisco
buckled and burned, New Orleans vanished,
the coasts of Asia were eaten by the sea.

And it will be on a day like this when the
solar system, the galaxy, the universe defy
all laws of nature, all reason, all sensibility.

It will be then that some few people will
metamorphose like a chrysalis opening, and
go on living at the Source of peace.

Preparation of the Bed

I found a four-inch planter pot,
took some crumbs of clay,
mixed them with compost
and a nugget of horse's waste.

This was a bed fit for an acorn,
and I slipped the acorn into it
with my finger pushing down
right to the second knuckle.
Then I filled the hole it left
and scrupulously tamped,
like tucking in a baby for the night.

But this was not for sleep.
This was to wake, and so it did,
first feeling out the depth below,
then reaching on all sides for food,
and finally erecting one thin
member toward the light,
leaves deploying as if it meant
to hear if there was life around.

At some point, when the time
felt right to coddle it no more,
I dug a hole and set it out
to grasp the planet and survive
on what the soil said,
the surplus of dark clouds,
the light from our communing star.

Working

Got a job with the governor, working around his house,
mowing the lawn, weeding the beds, painting.
I do a job, finish, clean up and just move on.

But when he has me work on one of the cars
I always want to take it for a drive, see how it runs.
Can't always do it. Sometimes he wants to use that one.

And it's worse when he says, "Teach my kid
how to swing a hammer," or "Show her how to shovel."
I do it best I know how, but I never get to see if it took.

Guess He doesn't care if I know, so I try to forget it.
But I always wonder why I don't care with some things
and do with others. My problem, I guess.

Kiss

The doe walks through my yard
as if it were her own.
And I suppose it is,
not being mine alone.

A useful fiction—that
we creatures can possess
in perpetuity
what's meant as one caress.

The laws of man are not
the laws of beast or God.
Who owns this cone of earth,
with stars and where He's trod?

My title to this land
will one day burn or mold
when this world's been transformed
or merely has been sold.

And yet my hope is that
what care I give in this
brief time I have to live
will linger like a kiss.

Lent II

Here we enter in this moist and darkened passageway,
A fitting entrance to the room beyond.
We've left behind the pond,
That futile mimic of the smiling sky,
To seek in darkness day,
And find that light, to live, must die.

We asked for something simple, something we could understand,
But all He gave were tales, a murky speech.
Peculiar way to teach.
We thought to go our way, admit we'd erred.
He made a dead man stand,
And did it with one making word.

The signs were past the force of men, and so we followed him.
But we mistook all might for what compels,
And then the proud chest swells,
Which makes a larger target for the foe.
Soon after, He turned grim,
Knowing some deadly undertow.

We'd never known that death and life could be related so,
But He revealed the boundary is thin.
To lose, then, is to win.
It seemed so false, but He had proved it true.
And yet our wrenching blow
Will be to some a stale review.

Give everything to those who have not yet fully matured
And they will yawn and say it's not enough.
You'll think my message gruff,

But teaching donkeys may require a club.
Ennui's not gently cured.
He could be gentle. He could be tough.

Wisdom

"I, Wisdom, dwell together with prudence; I possess knowledge and discretion.... I hate pride and arrogance, evil behavior and perverse speech."

PROVERBS 8 — 12–13

"The wise Christian is aware of God's immeasurable power, will, and affection while simultaneously working effectively and intelligently in the world."

DISCOVERING THE WAY OF WISDOM, EDWARD M. CURTIS AND JOHN J. BRUGALETTA

Everything Is Otherwise

With all the things I've ever learned to do—
grout tile, teach literature, appreciate my wife—
I learned it just as health and age said, Stop.

And sometimes, maybe the most crucial times,
success was just beyond my fingertips,
something I'd have grasped if I hadn't fallen dead.

But when I think of Socrates, told to commit suicide;
Lao-Tzu, his wisdom confiscated as he left China;
Da Vinci who hardly ever finished anything;

Lincoln's lead payment for preserving the nation;
and Jeshua assassinated by the Jerusalem He loved;
I begin to see that nothing succeeds if it succeeds.

The Iliad is left to scholars who seek their own fame,
and *Beowulf's* stern syllables survive as a flashy film.
Give us failure, and let it float away like a dead king.

Let me learn to respect my son's unpromising plans,
my daughter's disastrous choice of a husband,
and my neighbor's hatred of the things I say.

Fox Sparrow

I was just about to say the freeze
had turned the deck to fallen stars, when trees
reflected in a window light beguiled
a songbird into thinking it more wild
and knocked itself headfirst upon the pane
which uttered something like a sparrow slain.

A sort of sparrow's what it was, and so
there'd be enough on earth to let one go,
but this was mine. I'd been there when the sound
woke up the tom and brought that killer round
to see what windfall came to earth today,
an easy catch, and then the time of play.
He had within himself the urge to kill
that kept his ancestors alive, but still
enjoyed it even though he'd had his fill
that morning. So I took the bird in my
fleece robe and said, "It's over. Don't you die."

But die it did despite my ministrations,
caring, and Samaritan oblations.
And when I try to pick the one who erred,
I find myself as well as cat and bird.
What sort of reformation would suffice
to turn this world around and make it nice?

The frosty glint is off my deck for now
but will return. We'll make it through somehow.

Awe

"Touching your cap to the squire may be . . . bad
for the squire, but it's . . . good for you."
                              J.R.R. Tolkien

We who are bereft of stately kings,
who judge each unmet person equal to
ourselves, but separate, and impotent
to tell us how we ought to live our lives,
who think ourselves courageous to deny
superiors at work a "yes" or "sir";
who grudge the admiration due the great;
we prideful insects lack the protocol
to speak to One for whom our learned books
are like the simple scratches toddlers make
when first they hold a crayon to a page.

Our skulls contain no lobes for dignity,
(except our own, and none believes in that),
so majesty, the earthly kind, none can abide
(except when singing, and that's only rote).
Our souls have shrunk, these latter days, so small
there is too little room for You inside.

Expand them, Lord, till we're magnanimous.
Though Christ threw wide your doors and waved us in,
teach us to tremble as we wipe our feet.

Well Water

The well collapsed and so we had to move
our water shaft a dozen miles away.
The case was either that or learn to love
a glass of sand. We couldn't move the sky.

I thought, "This is a prompt to find the spot
where living water will rise up and flow,
where heaven's rain will trickle, concentrate
and wait for us, a thing both old and new."

But everywhere we dug the holes were dry,
the grass was dying, blossoms all gone limp.
How long could this go on and not destroy
our will and force us to displace our camp?

Are we best fitted for a roving life
of stubborn camels, smoking fires—reduced
to what, some thousand years ago, we left
behind: our weakened elders who knew best.

There is no answer but to trudge along
to search for what may slake our raging thirst.
It may be where a good man has been hanged
in deft reversal of what seemed a farce.

Born Again

The man they like to emulate had said
a good reception where He lives depends
on being born again. And so they tell
of summer camp as kids, or campus groups,
or tent revivals and an altar call—
they "handed over all they had to Christ."

And I believed them, but it's puzzling when
they place such weight on what their houses cost,
or sometimes feel great pride in what they know,
or wish to keep their health, their youth, their hair.

A birth is leaving (for one's life) the womb,
the customary comforts and the warmth,
a place to lay one's head. It means to pass
one's brain case through an opening so small
the bony mind must change its shape or die.

It means a change so scary that we weep,
but weeping starts our breathing. Then we meet
the beings we had only known by voice:
she has a smell, he gives a scratchy kiss.

Look, Ananias and Sapphira died.

Containers

Forgive us, Lord, the modules of our thought,
premeasured, uniform, accepted, bought.
"Choose medium or large in taupe or black";
It's "what they're wearing," and it's in the sack.

We're woefully behind the times unless
the current topics are the ones we bless.
We draw neat lines between our foe and friend
when You yourself said wait until the end.

We're either right and brown or left and pink;
we have no sympathy with those who think
that both sides see some facts and make some sense
yet strain their insights for a strong defense.

We think we think, and seem to know we know,
until some Socrates has stooped so low
as to explain our ignorance and force
our logic back to view its bogus source.

Sometimes we try to know You as a friend,
but how can simple being apprehend
that angry love, caress that uncreates,
who box their oranges in cornered crates,

much less who look for lions with a cage
that would not hold the tabby's minor rage.
Assuming we can stretch and still be yours,
widen our walls, we pray, enlarge our doors.

That, if we may not hold You all in all,
we may invite You in our vastest hall
and there receive your smallest finger's end.
Then we might mean it when we call You friend.

Belief

turn

For thousands of years a stream of minds has worked
at casting the grains of theology up where the breeze
could pluck the heretical husks from the seed,
depositing wheat like manna at our bent knees.

It was divine, the Wind that winnowed our notions,
not of a personal bent or random emotions.
Are we then to seek, pursue and treasure this dross
where it litters the fields and berms, clasping our loss
to our breast instead of the true way of the cross?

counter-turn

It all is pendant from the breeze that winnowed thoughts.
Was that the Spirit's will? If so, it acted
through a witch's brew of potions and garrotes,
conniving, lies and politics, all enacted
in assurance that it kept and grew the church,
no matter that it would Christ's name besmirch.

And out of this, a tame and lukewarm creed
for which some few contribute but would never bleed.
Yet we are placid, our salvation guaranteed.

stand

The mind is easy when its choice is clearly two,
the views of others and the ones you hold as true.
It strains no one's judgment to see himself as right,
no matter that his beliefs would form a blight
if cloned and spread throughout this sapient sphere.
The real is never neat; it's somewhat queer.

It's best to pick a pair or three to heed,
then pray for wisdom to complete your creed.

CPAP

"And breathed into his nostrils the breath of life;
and man became a living thing." Genesis 2 — 7

There comes a time, a rending time,
when most of us awaken to the fact
that we are dead, and every act
is worth the tenth part of a dime.

"Dead," we say, and though we are,
we wish for God to rid us of death's curse.
Then comes a gadget like a nurse
and gives us breath like puffing a cigar.

How packed would churches be if these
were marketed as Holy Ghost machines,
available alike to thugs or deans,
inspiring them for twenty bucks per wheeze.

The imps in hell would sport and frisk
to learn we earthly fools might take
this plastic pump for God—a fake
whose kiss lulls like a basilisk.

Purpose

Some are certain they believe
everything the Bible tells.
Others harbor some old peeve
with ecclesiastic swells.

I am sure of nothing pat,
save that I'm not sure of much.
Controversies? Much bird scat.
This has kept me out of touch.

I prefer this, for I think
that which lures the flock to pews
will, when comprehended, stink—
all except for sincere News.

Some will see religious need
as a chance genetic quirk
passed along by human seed
worthy of the skeptic's smirk.

That may be, and if it's so,
humans are a rare disease,
earth's unique inapropos,
demigod but also sleaze.

I prefer to guess we're here
as a bold experiment:
will we fumble as did Lear,
or live nobly as did Kent?

Those who think they surely know
likely have not searched the roots
seeking for support below
while above they bear small fruits.

But the strongest human drive
is to wear some uniform
making us, not just alive,
but within or out the norm.

So the "inners" gather tribes
into large confederations,
while each "outer" soon subscribes
to all trendy bifurcations.

If I'd made such clever apes,
giving them a brain to reason,
I'd have kicked those jackanapes
into hell for outright treason.

But the One, if there, is waiting
for some reason no one knows,
while we lordlings go on hating
anyone who wears odd clothes.

I'd say time and space are dead,
but a dead man came to life.
This of course has been gainsaid
for the sake of causing strife.

I could surely disbelieve
were it not for this event,
but I'm forced to be naive
by all reason's firm assent.

So I speak in solitude
to an Absence (so it seems),
and at last I must conclude
somewhere hidden something gleams.

Oracular Meddling

The broker strains to know tomorrow's price
and weathermen sift data for a peek
at whether we will wake to sun or ice.
It all becomes less clear as seers seek
to see ahead a few days or a week.
What will our children's children come to be?
Will time turn things more rosy tinged or bleak?
The world is filled with blind men who would see.

Etruscans practiced beastly sacrifice,
then read the future in a spot or streak,
while others ciphered stars or threw the dice.
King Saul insisted Samuel's ghost should speak
and learned that very soon his corpse would reek.
We are not chained, but neither are we free
to know the future through a slick technique.
We want to know, but dislike what we see.

We're less like eagles than we are like mice,
brave in our holes, but at the heights more meek.
And so to melt our spines we beg a nice
long view to where the earth will shriek
and geysers grow into a deadly peak,
or huge subductions send a killing sea.
There's no good reason for a fit of pique.
We hate our blindness and we loathe to see.

We'd ask an oracle if we were Greek,
then tear our hair at what the gods foresee.
This little disk of light holds eyes oblique,
protecting us from what we may not see.

Don Quixote the Chickadee

This chickadee insists that he must throw
himself against the glass as if insane.
I'm sure he thinks he's jousting with his foe,
a base intruder mostly in his brain.

Presuming that a shift in light will turn
this feathered knight into a pacifist,
I flick a switch to make the room's light burn
but still he thinks his rival must exist.

And so I leave him to his *idée fixe*,
for even God has left such ones alone
with rampant hubris that in heaven reeks
and causes seraphim to wince and groan.

The rest of us know mere appearance may
disturb our spirits when the light's at play.

Silence

I.
The burglar never caught, the cop gone bad
protected by his friends, husbands cheating,
potentates turned vicious or plain mad—
a silence from the skies will have them bleating
that there's no God, no gently ruling mind,
no good that everywhere is truly good,
no universal truth that we can find,
(and oh how inconvenient if we could).
All this from silence. Some will hold their tongues.
Is it from wisdom or a lack of lungs?

II.
The master who has turned and walked away
has not attained a non-existent state.
He might have seen that nothing he could say
would heal your eyes or dissipate your hate.
It's possible, of course, your life is lost,
for you've refused the only offer made.
You have your freedom, and this is the cost.
He gave you love, which you've somewhere mislaid.
If I'm mistaken, you are truly blest,
but nothing that I've said was said in jest.

III.
The keenest tool will sometimes slip and cut
the hand that wields it if the wood is wry.
But only master teachers will apply
a silence that allows the proud to strut.
Those who must chatter when the student errs
will hear the same if they should step astray,

which would mean constant quibbling every day.
From this the better sort of sage demurs.
The method holds some risk. The student might
learn nothing from his waywardness but spite.
But grown-ups must not fear to walk at night.

Led into the Wilderness

After you have declared your loyalty to God,
and after an all-too-brief honeymoon,
He will determine how deep the roots have sunk,
those stabilizing roots of your glib words.

You declared your loyalty in an orderly room;
now you are being led into chaos and confusion.
There are no markers, no points of reference,
no map on a kiosk saying, "You are here."
Only one thing orients you—a tract, instructions.

Some of you will not accept instructions easily.
Others will obey them so cleverly that
they will not feel obliged to obey them at all.

But those who discover in themselves a hunger,
an ache and a longing for any sound or sign
from Him will press His words to their lips,
savor the bread of them, chew and swallow them.

In digesting His way of being, His wisdom
and His kindness, His firm hold on a reality
that you would never have thought real before,
you speak only possible answers in the wilderness,
answers to the quick temptations, the quick fix,
the sword of Alexander splitting the knot
instead of the tedious work of raveling out
the tough dilemmas of a problem-planted earth.

Surprised by the Ease of It

"Do not be overrighteous, neither be overwise. . ..
Do not be overwicked, and do not be a fool. . ..
The one who fears God will avoid all extremes."
                                        Ecclesiastes

My bedroom window looked to the fig tree
that scented our back yard with its ripe fruits.
It stood with its arms held upward all its life,
but its fruiting toil was its simultaneous prayer.
I sometimes stared out that window into the
blinding Arizona sunlight and thought I saw
what then I had no name for, and now can only
tag ineptly with the borrowed sound "Shekinah."

No eighteen-year-old tells of such visions to those
who work in grease and fumes for little pay,
or manage homes without a syllable of thanks.
And so I went to books, those silent sages,
letting the black seeds of their words sprout in me,
at length to form in me a skin of righteousness
and afterward a longing to be extremely wise.

If I knew anything worthwhile, I knew the popular
had compromised the truth, and only truth
withstands repeated falls and in the end arises.
I saw at last that I was right at first:
Qoheleth spoke the wisdom that transcends
a human urge to bribe the gods, or to
propitiate the one true God. We are to live, to work,
to fruit, to shy at each extreme, to love
the taste of figs, to live exactly as the thing that we

were muscled and were nerved to be.
This is obedience. This is devotion's prayer.

Yes, No, and Neither

Every dawn is different and the same.
Wood will build but wood will also burn.
Humans can be wild as wolves or tame.
Women will adhere to men or spurn.
The world is serious; the world's a game.

We cheer our tribes as did Neanderthals,
yet some can think and judge and weigh.
We laud our freedom and enjoy our thralls.
We see in black or white but know of gray.
We walk upright so we can take more falls.

What is this life that cherishes ideals
requiring amputation of some limb?
Why were we born surviving on our meals
if we must be fastidious and prim?
Our brain is baffled and our heart congeals.

There is a naiveté we only dream
that imitates the newborn's placid stare
but is substantial as a puff of steam.
Like it or not, we have become aware
that life is still and changing as a stream.

Naming the Logos

Though trees are ragged, every building's plumb.
We see the world and wish it fit our mind
the way a grapefruit's segments fit their rind,
but quarks and toadstools only leave me dumb.
The word I most desire will never come.

Tell me why earth should intersect with hay.
And what have oaks to do with apple trees,
or cactus blossoms with the needful bees?
Does thinking know, or does it only play?
The phrase I want to say I never say.

The best the world contains is so remote,
my hands fit nothing and my lips are dry.
I take two breaths, then on the third I die.
We're most precise at what our words connote.
The only name I love eludes my throat.

Finis

That wispy day we hardly see
is like a road trip when the haze,
as we approach, turns out to be
the mountains that betoken days
when we will weaken and our throats
will stutter like a billy goat's.

We'll walk bent over, locust-like,
and if we're able, love the child
who ran into us on his bike,
for we were once that young, that wild.
What shall we wish for on that dawn
when light goes dim and earth will yawn?

Proper Prophet

When I awake to cock-crow in the night
and darkness lies like mold on sleeping life,
I lie in bed and think, beside my wife,
of time to come, and children, and no light.

"This silly bird, in iridescent pride,
is wishing for the sun to make him shine.
His voice, like lightning, cuts a puny line
across the face of blackness." And I lied.

Soon after, morning came. It always had.
This bird, this proper prophet, saw the sun.
I saw what I could touch: This trend, that fad.

Remember, mind, those cries when worlds are dun.
All lies are darkness. (Darkness lies, "All's mad.")
I see now light and truth and life are one.

www.ingramcontent.com/pod-product-compliance
Lightning Source LLC
Chambersburg PA
CBHW070322100426
42743CB00011B/2523